My Arrival to (and Early Life in) New York City

New York City, Volume 6

DeLynn Nicole Poma

Published by DeLynn Nicole Poma, 2023.

While every precaution has been taken in the preparation of this book, the publisher assumes no responsibility for errors or omissions, or for damages resulting from the use of the information contained herein.

MY ARRIVAL TO (AND EARLY LIFE IN) NEW YORK CITY

First edition. September 5, 2023.

Copyright © 2023 DeLynn Nicole Poma.

ISBN: 979-8223397007

Written by DeLynn Nicole Poma.

Table of Contents

My Arrival to (and Early Life in) New York City

DeLynn Nicole Poma (Written in 2002)

Introduction:

This book is about my early beginnings in New York City. It talks about the people I met, the challenges I faced, and the difficulty I had establishing myself in this place. I thought I was going to take the city by storm, but it seems to have swept me away instead. Though I try to understand my mind at the time, I can only come as close as my recollection of it. The real story is told by the letters & journals I wrote at that time. Alas, this serves as a snapshot description.

This is a combination piece & includes these previously self-published titles:

Chapter 01: "<u>My Arrival to New York City</u>"

Chapter 02: "<u>My First Night in New York City</u>"

Chapter 03: "<u>My Early Days in New York City</u>"

Chapter 04: "<u>My Early Years in New York City</u>"

Chapter 05: "<u>My Adjustment to Life in New York</u>"

Dedication:

This is dedicated to John, the man I met my first night in New York City. This is also dedicated to the others who took me in and housed me at the time (most notably, Ray and another John). I'm thankful for the kindness of strangers.

BLANK PAGE

Chapter 01: My Arrival to New York City

New York City, December 1993. This is the first picture taken of me in N.Y.C. I never smiled
and I always wore black. I'm in Central Park; you can see Wollman Rink directly behind me.

[This is the story of how I arrived at New York City. It describes my experience of starting a new life inside the mega-metropolis that is N.Y.C. No doubt this was a rough-and-tumble time in my life. At this time, I eagerly pursued the music scene and tried out for various pop/rock bands. I went to bars and clubs, and because I didn't want to give my real name, I introduced myself as "Violet." I arrived at the tender age of 21 and survived the hard knocks of this big city for 15 years.]

It was the week before Halloween, in October of 1993, when I arrived by Greyhound to the Port Authority bus terminal smack in the middle of New York City. I was just 21 years old. I had $125 dollars in my pocket and 2 tote bags. That was all. I didn't know anybody; I didn't have a job lined up, and I didn't have a place to stay. Some say I was daring and very brave; others say I was senseless and stupid, and perhaps both could be true. I suppose an element of innocence and naiveté could have been part of the package as well. I was young and bold, just 21 years old, and ready to take on the world and to take the city by storm. Yet, in hindsight, it seems to have swept me away instead.

I came from Michigan, but I did not come to New York directly from there. I headed first for Atlanta, Georgia, and spent a near year down there. I had left Michigan on a bright and sunny April afternoon and drove to Atlanta in my little white Chevette. I could say that I came to New York from Atlanta, but that would not be true either: because I stayed briefly in Nashville, Tennessee with a friend I had at the time, and it was from there that I rode the bus to New York.

To begin with, I have to know why I left Michigan in the first place. Discovering that reason should be simple, but it is not. I honestly don't know what made me leave so hastily and improvised, unrehearsed and ill-prepared, except to say that I felt compelled: I felt propelled on the inside. Not only was I driven by something inside me, but also, I was drawn by something outside of myself. I can't pinpoint what drew me so strongly. I can only say that it felt like it was a magnetic force that pulled me out without the possibility of my resisting.

MY ARRIVAL TO NEW YORK CITY

BLANK PAGE

Chapter 02: My First Night in New York City

DeLynn Nicole Poma (New York City) March 1994, Original and Unfiltered Image.

SHORT INTRO:

[I understand that I busted in a bit roughshod, but we live in a very different world today than we did in the early nineties. Don't forget: This was the year 1993. The amount of information on the Internet, and the easy-and-everywhere utilization of it (and access to it) via both cellular telephone and desktop (or laptop) computer (or tablet) did not exist back then. If you wanted a job in another state, you had to move there first; there were no job ads to be found and applied to "online." If you wanted to find a room for rent, a roommate, or a living situation of some kind, you had to search for fliers and posters plastered on walls in public places or look through advertisements posted in the Classified section of the local newspaper. We had "land lines" back then, and if you were cool, you had a "beeper" or a pager. I didn't have an e-mail address let alone a mobile/cell phone. If I was not at home, then I wouldn't know someone called until I got home and checked the answering machine for a message/voicemail. When I was out, I relied on payphones to make the calls. They were everywhere (even in subway stations) and, in Manhattan, you could find a payphone on every street corner – and you could make a call for just a quarter! By the time I left N.Y.C. 15 years later, there were no more payphones; they had entirely disappeared. If I had today's technology at my disposal those many years ago, this story would never have been written. I would have been able to find everything that I needed online and made all arrangements prior to my arrival. Alas, I was just 21 years old, and this is how I began my life in this great big city.]

I REMEMBER MY FIRST night in New York City as clear as day. I had hoped to arrive in the afternoon in order to give myself a little time to seek out a place to stay before nightfall. But due to bus delays, I didn't actually arrive until around 10 o'clock that night. By then, the city's lights were lit up bright and all aglow. I could see them from my dirty bus window. They were truly beautiful: like stars resting on the earth, and the sight of the city from afar filled me with a sense of awe and anticipation. I planned to look up advertisements for rooms for rent once we pulled into the bus station. But then as we got closer in, I saw all the trash and graffiti, and looking out upon my new surroundings, I was suddenly gripped with fear and dread.

That's when I started talking to the passenger next to me. I asked her if she might know of a place to stay. She told me to ask around for an inexpensive room for rent as soon as we pulled into Port Authority. Another passenger overheard our conversation and offered to take me to his mother's place for the night. I declined at first and said I should find a shelter to stay for a night or two until I could establish a permanent living arrangement. But judging from the stories I was hearing, and from the things he was telling me, shelters were not safe places. He said me being young, small, and female, that I would probably be beaten up, and that my stuff was sure to get stolen. I figured staying with somebody's mom would be my best bet.

I put my two tote bags in a locker when we arrived at Port Authority. My mind was circling a mile a minute as I saw so many people buzzing all around me. I got on a train with the guy I met on the bus and was absolutely fascinated by the concept of the subway: to be traveling so quickly in a dark tunnel underground was truly a marvel for me. He said he had to run an errand first. He took me to Harlem and left me on a street corner, saying he'd be right back. I watched him walk away and wondered if he would come back, and what I would do if he didn't. Then a car alarm went off and three guys started fighting with each other. It scared me, because I was alone and didn't know where else to go. I went inside a building and continued to wait, but the security guard there told me to leave. I asked if I could stand inside the doorway for a while, but he would not let me. I stood outside feeling frightened until my bus-friend came back. His returning surprised me; I was thankful and relieved. I hoped that he would take me to his mother's place. Instead, he suggested we go to a night club. Once again, I went with him, because I didn't know where else to go. On our way towards the subway station, I saw a homeless man set a trash can on fire, and I was mesmerized by the blaze.

We took a train to the East Village and arrived at CBGB. Once there, he led me to a table and told me he was going to get us some drinks. I kept my attention fixated and focused on the band that was performing on stage, and didn't notice him walk out the door. After awhile, I began to wonder what was taking him so long. I thought he forgot where I sat, so I got up to look for him and soon discovered he was nowhere to be found. I should have expected that he would ditch me. I was just someone he met on the bus and it wasn't as if he had an obligation to help me. I went outside and stood there for awhile wondering what I should do. I started to ask some women if they knew of a room for rent, and hoped one of them might be able to direct me, or at least give me a good lead. But instead of being kindly received, I was either rudely shrugged off or simply ignored, and once more I was at a loss as to what to do.

I went back inside and asked someone how I could get back to Port Authority. That's when I met Mike. He worked the lights. I explained my situation, to which he suggested that I crash with him for the night. I declined and said I should just go back to Port Authority. My hope was that once there my luck would change, and that I would find out about a cheap room to rent advertised on one of the bulletin boards. So he said he'd be there late into the night and for me to come back if I changed my mind. I was already changing my mind as I walked out the door. I knew that I didn't have much money, and if I blew it on a room, I would be left with nothing. But then I knew that I did this before: I experienced this and made it through. I spent my money on motel rooms and got down to my last $20 bucks, but then met Billy (my old roommate in Atlanta) and found a job just in time. I figured that if I could just get back to Port Authority, then I could create a constructive plan of action. Perhaps I could find advertisements posted up on walls and establish an arrangement of some kind – or maybe I might just catch the next bus out of New York after all.

I went back outside and asked someone to show me the way back to the Port Authority Bus Station, but instead of pointing me north, they pointed me west. So I crossed Bowery Street and walked down Bleecker Street towards Broadway. Yet as I walked, I started to feel a sense of belonging to the city, and it began to feel as if New York City was truly my home. Although I was filled with so much confusion and fear, I was already feeling the excitement and energy from the busy city streets, and I knew that I very much wanted to stay.

That's when I passed by a group of 3 guys standing by a fire escape. I was struck by the way the tall one with blonde hair stopped talking when he saw me. I don't even attract to blondes, but he looked at me as if he knew me, and suddenly my heart filled with utter desperation. I knew I made a mistake coming here the way I did, and that I had put myself in a dangerous position, but I had come too far to turn back now. So I stopped to talk to the blonde guy in the black leather jacket. I got a feeling from him, though I am unable to explain exactly what it was. It was just something inside me telling me that he was safe and would not bring me to harm. So when he asked me where I was headed, I said I was on my way back to Port Authority in the hopes to find flyers or other advertisements about a temporary (but available immediately!) room for rent or other living arrangement. In the course of our conversation, I conveyed that I was eager and desperate for a shelter situation of some kind. That's when he offered to take me in. He let me stay with him for that night.

MY ARRIVAL TO NEW YORK CITY

We walked down Bleecker Street towards Broadway and went to a Mexican eatery that showcases salsa bands called "Gonzalez y Gonzalez" on Mercer Street. I told him how I had come and why I wanted to be here. I said New York to me was a place of vibrancy and vitality, and it was the exact place that I desired to be. I said that I came to pursue my music dream and I wanted to sing in a pop/rock band. He simply listened to me relate my tale. He had already introduced me to his friends and he said his name was John.

Once we arrived at the restaurant, we sat down at the bar. He ordered me cranberry juice and gave me a bowl of chips to snack on. He asked if I was hungry, but I didn't want to be any more imposing than I already was, so I said no. I'm not sure if he noticed that I finished the entire bowl. We hung out for awhile before taking a taxi back to his studio apartment that was located in the mid-30's on Lexington Avenue. I distinctly remember this, because I was watching the street signs, and when he said his building number, he just told the cab driver that it was on "Lex Ave." I had never been in a yellow city taxi before, and I was struck by the craziness of the city streets. When we entered his small apartment, he gave me a towel so I could take a shower, a shirt to sleep in, and a blanket to sleep with. I made my bed on the couch and fell asleep.

It was about 3 A.M. when I woke up because I felt cold. It had turned chilly in the night, and he had left the window open. I got up to shut it, but before I did, I stuck my head outside and noticed taxis still on the streets, and quite a few pedestrians who walked up and down and in between them. I stood there for a long moment just listening to the shouts and laughter; feeling the life, energy and excitement that they exuded. At that moment, I decided that I was going to stay no matter what hard knocks or hard times were coming my way. I knew I had found my "heart's home" and I was never going to leave.

Then I tried to shut the window, but it got stuck. I would have simply gone back to sleep, but it was too cold. I kept trying to shut it and it squeaked, and that was when I woke up John. I told him I was cold, so he got up and shut the window for me. He went back to sleep and I returned to my little bed on the couch. The next day, I went back to Port Authority to retrieve my belongings. John walked with me for part of the way, then he wished me good luck and we both went our own ways. And I never saw him again after that.

When I arrived at Port Authority, I retrieved my two tote bags and bought a newspaper. Having made it through the night, the new day was a fresh beginning. I felt optimistic and determined to make this city my home. There were to be difficult and even dangerous events up ahead, but I didn't know that then. All I knew was that leaving or simply giving up was not an option. There was excitement in my heart. I anticipated something, yet I didn't know what that was. Still, I felt a true sense of purpose, like there was a reason for me to be here. It was as if something had pulled me like a magnet into this city, and that very same thing held me fixed in its grip and firm in its grasp.

MY ARRIVAL TO NEW YORK CITY

BLANK PAGE

Chapter 03: My Early Days in New York City

Roosevelt Island, New York (June 1995). I'm not trying to look sexy:
I'm holding back my hair away from my face – it was a windy day!

[GETTING STARTED AND establishing a new life in New York was by no means an easy feat. This is what it was like for me during those early days in the big city.]

MY ARRIVAL TO NEW YORK CITY

My decision to stay in the city was definite upon that first night, and although my mind was made up and my heart firmly resolved, my ability to find available and affordable housing kept my settling here in a perpetual state of uncertainty. The most immediate problem I had to contend with was that I had no money. The $125 bucks I brought with me soon slipped through my fingers. In this city, it was more like spare change. I didn't have a job and I was not at all acquainted with the city to know the ins and outs of how things work here.

After that first night I spent with John, I stayed with Mike, the man I met at CBGB. Mike lived in an art-loft space with four other guys near the Lorimer Street station stop off the L-train in Brooklyn. I stayed with all five of them for about two weeks. They each had made their own make-shift bedrooms with built-in walls and doors. A couple of rooms had only curtains for doors, and one person just slept in an open space. Since there was no place to put me, they gave me the couch. I was sleeping on yet another couch, but I didn't mind. I'd be happy sleeping on floors so long as I have a roof over my head. There was no need to store my stuff, because all I had were those two tote bags. I kept them underneath my couch-bed.

I don't remember much about that time, although I do recall there being a huge swing that hung from the ceiling. It was situated next to the pool table. I'm very fond of swings. It has something to do with my fascination with the perpetual motion of going back and forth, and my enchantment with the incessant movement of swinging at a steady rhythm. One night, while Mike and his friend were playing pool, I joined their company and made myself comfy on the swing. I reminisce those feelings of happiness just swinging while watching the boys play. It was during rare moments such as those where I felt a real sense of hope that things would work out for me, and that it all would turn out okay.

I knew my time with Mike would be short, because I couldn't expect him to continue putting me up. He did have four other roommates to consider, and he couldn't let me stay without their consent. I looked for a living situation through the Village Voice. I noticed an ad for a room for rent in the upper part of Manhattan in the area known as Inwood, which is located at the northern tip of the island. It's so far north, that one can look out over the river and see the residential buildings of The Bronx. The ad caught my eye mostly because of its relatively cheap price. Yet I was also a little curious by the words "Christian male seeks Christian female to share apartment." I found it strange, but thought to check it out, because it did make him sound as if he would at least be honest.

I called him up and we spoke briefly over the telephone. We scheduled a time to meet and he gave me the directions to his place. On the set day, I took the A-train to the very last stop in Manhattan. I walked to 215th Street and came to his apartment building. I took the elevator up to the fifth floor and knocked on his door. He opened it with a bright smile on his face and was dressed in his business suit. He shook my hand, said his name was Ray, and welcomed me in. Then he showed me around the apartment and said he was planning to give the woman the bedroom, and that he would make the living-room his own sleeping quarters.

After showing me the place, he offered to order Chinese food. He asked me to join him, and as I hadn't eaten all day, I readily agreed to accompany him in his Chinese dining. We ate chicken-fried rice, drank Coca-Cola, and talked for over 2 hours. He told me about his work at a computer company and his desire to start his own business. He had a friend who wanted to start up a business with him and make it a partnership. The two of them planned to build and repair computers both commercially and for private clients. He also talked about his family, mentioning how he wasn't close to any of them. We kept talking like old friends and it was an unusual feeling for me. It was as though we had known each other for a long time. I showed interest in sharing the apartment already knowing that I couldn't afford it. I said I would call to let him know for sure. He agreed to wait, brought me my coat, and bid me goodnight.

MY ARRIVAL TO NEW YORK CITY

All I had to do was find work, yet I was having a hard time doing that. It was unusual for me not to be able to land a job. I was always able to find one immediately back in Michigan, but here it seemed employers didn't want to hire someone from a small Midwestern town with no Bachelor's Degree (at that time) and no "New York experience" as they called it. This really frustrated me, because I had plenty of work experience, just not in New York. I had asked a few employers what the difference was between my work experience and that of New York, and one woman said that it is just not the same. Things are much more fast-paced, she said, and demand a higher volume. *A small town in Michigan simply doesn't compare,* she said with snobbery in her voice. I swear she held her nose a little too high in the air. My job search continued to be a constant pounding of the pavement, with one rejection after another. I hoped to change my circumstance, but the job situation remained grim.

I went to retail stores but many of them were not hiring. The few with signs in their windows would still tell me they weren't hiring. I filled out countless applications for retail jobs but never heard a word from any of them. I went to restaurants, to bars and clubs, but they, too, would coin that "New York work experience" to me. I went to temporary agencies for something administrative (like answering a telephone) and filled out all the extensive paperwork, but nothing panned out. I would call only to hear:

"*Nothing today, but try back tomorrow.*" I'd call tomorrow and hear:

"*Nothing yet, but try next week.*" I'd try again that next week and get:

"*Still nothing. But as soon as something opens up, we'll give you a call.*"

They never did. It got to the point where I started to seriously doubt not only my work experience and abilities, but also my own sense of competence. I received so much rejection during those first few years from both potential employers and possible roommates that it was as if it were coming from some inexhaustible source in the sky. The rejections seemed limitless, thereby causing my sense of optimism and determination to plummet into an unknown abyss. The confidence in my capabilities appeared to take a headlong plunge into a deep and bottomless pit.

Then before I knew it, my allotted time-frame had passed, and Mike wasn't sure if he could let me stay any longer. For it wasn't his space alone, and there were four other roommates to contend with. So I continued my search for yet another place to stay, couch to crash on, and hardwood floor to call my bed. I thought about Ray and entertained the notion of paying rent at the end of the month. I asked Mike for his advice, and he told me not to call him, because he most likely cannot be trusted. He said a Christian man would not be seeking a Christian woman unless he wanted more than just a roommate. It seemed he had a point there, for it did appear rather peculiar for a man to be seeking a woman as a living partner to share his space when he only had one bedroom. I began to question why he wasn't seeking another Christian man. Even Mike agreed with me, and he was an atheist. Therefore, I decided that it wasn't a good idea to move in with Ray. I assumed from this that he had hidden intentions.

Yet at the same time, he was so warm and welcoming towards me, and he even extended his home if ever I were in need. He felt like an old friend, like someone I already knew and trusted, though we just met. But I took Mike's advice and decided not to take the room; besides, I couldn't afford it anyway. But because I said I would get back to him with my decision, I called him. I said I wouldn't be taking the room, but thanked him for a most enjoyable evening. He asked me to keep his phone number and to call if ever I were in need. I kept his information in my little wallet and continued on with my search.

Mike didn't want to just send me back out on the street, so he put me up with his neighbor who lived down the hall for another week. I was very grateful for that. I kept my hopes ever so high that my situation would change drastically, dramatically, within the week. But those seven days seemed to speed by in just seven seconds. Nothing changed, and again I felt that feeling once more of hopelessness and despondency.

That's when I met David. His band was looking for a singer. I went to his practice studio and sang, but I was off on most of the notes. I don't have an ear for pitch at all. Soon we stopped (because he could see I wasn't what they were looking for) and started talking. I said I was from Michigan and came to New York to pursue my music dream: I wanted to make a demo and get a record deal. He asked where I lived, and I said I was still working on that. I know how it must have sounded: Surely my situation seemed outlandish; my predicament farfetched. For here I was with no job, no money, and no housing or permanent place to live. But it was the truth; it was my life at that time.

He then asked how I could have come to New York like that, but I didn't have an answer. For I myself don't understand what I must have been thinking. If I had been a drug user, I'd say that I came to New York when I was on a high. Or if I lived in an abusive situation, I'd say that I came to the city to escape it, but none of that was true. I'm not sure I'll ever know what drove me here so strongly or what tugged me from within. I was so young, and though I had the guts to simply step out, take off and go, I didn't use my head to adequately plan the transition, and I should not have come so irrationally and ill-prepared.

He offered to let me stay for a couple weeks until I was able to get on my feet. He lived in Park Slope with his father and an older brother, with whom he shared a bedroom. But his brother was away at the time, so he gave me his bed to sleep in. During those two weeks, he gave me tokens to use the subway and made sure I was fed. I used my time as wisely as I could. I answered ads for jobs, went on a few interviews, and pounded the pavement until all my energy was entirely exhausted. Two weeks had passed and I still hadn't landed a job.

One night, David and I sat in the living-room talking and watching late night T.V. He flipped a few channels and we tuned into "<u>Tales from the Crypt</u>." It was a spooky little show that came on at 12 A.M. every Saturday and a personal favorite of mine. After that, there was "<u>Elvira – Mistress of the Dark</u>," but we didn't make it for that one. Instead, we got into a serious discussion. He said I should go back to Michigan and offered to pay the plane ticket for my return. Although my predicament appeared impossible, I didn't want to just give up, but I knew I couldn't stay with him any longer, even before he said so. I was a stranger after all, and he was under no obligation to continue providing for me.

It was then that he gave me an ultimatum: Either I accept a return ticket back to the Midwest or be put back out on the street. It seemed cruel at the time, and it really angered me, but now that I look back on it, I can see that he didn't know what more he could do. I think he thought that he hadn't any other choice. I remember feeling my heart sink to the pit of my stomach. He just assumed I would accept the return ticket. I couldn't miss the look of shock on his face when I said I would find a way to stay in New York, even if I slept out on the street. Something began screaming inside me. It wasn't possible for me to return home, because I was already home. It was New York that drew me: I was magically and magnetically drawn to this city. This was where I wanted to be.

It was well past Midnight when I put on my thin jacket and picked up my two tote bags. I went outside into the cold rain and found a payphone. I searched my wallet for Ray's phone number because he said I could call him if ever I were in need. Moments passed as I stood there getting wet and cold, while giving it a final thought. All I could see was every door closing in on me. In my desperation, I picked up the phone and called Ray. I must've woke him up from his sleep, because I noticed a scratchiness in his voice that usually accompanies those moments of just waking. I'm not sure what I said, but I must have adequately conveyed my desperate situation. I wasn't going back or giving up, that much I knew. I would sooner sleep out in the rain.

Ray suggested I should come over. So I took the F-train (orange line) from 7th Avenue in Brooklyn to Jay Street/Borough Hall. From there I transferred to the A-train (blue line). I took it uptown all the way to the last stop in Manhattan and walked the rest of the way. I don't remember what I was thinking; I only recall knocking on his door and him having waited up for me. We didn't say much to each other that night. He already had prepared a bed for me on the living-room couch. I set down my two tote bags as he hung up my thin wet jacket. He then bid me goodnight and then went to his own bedroom to sleep.

The next morning, he got up early to go to work. I was already awake, and I could hear his muffled sounds as he got ready to leave. I rested awhile longer before getting up, as I didn't know what to get up for. Here I was in another man's apartment, sleeping on another couch, and with all my personal belongings and possessions crammed into those two tote bags. By now, I was practically and entirely out of money. In fact, I really was out of money: It was David who had given me the token to get to Ray's.

I honestly could not see how all of this was going to work out. I couldn't see any light at the end of this tunnel. I just knew that I desperately wanted it to. I realized that if I were to make it through all of this, then I could make it through anything. At least that much I knew. Things could only get better. But when things would start to get better was the question.

BLANK PAGE

22

Chapter 04: My Early Years in New York City

Short Intro:

[If I thought getting started in New York was tough, getting settled in this city proved to be an even harder challenge. I desperately wanted to stay, but I honestly didn't think I'd be able to pull that off. This is what life was like for me in my "turbulent twenties" and those early years in the concrete jungle of N.Y.C.]

Times Square, New York. DeLynn Poma, June 1995.

Times Square, New York. DeLynn, June 1995.

A Lot of Hard Times, A Little Bit of Magic

This is "Wigstock" in July of 1995. (This guy was really funny!)

MY FIRST THREE YEARS in New York City consisted of mostly struggle and difficulty. As Patty Griffin sings in one of her songs: *"a lot of hard times, a little bit of magic..."* But for the most part, I had feelings of emptiness and hopelessness, inadequacy and despondency that seemed to surround and overwhelm me. Fear and despair became a permanent part of my existence as well. It was as if a big cloud of misery hovered over me, like one massive gray mass of utter unhappiness. Things were so difficult for me. It seemed my efforts were always in vain. Nothing ever worked out, and everything I touched turned to dust.

These were my desperate days, where I would have done just about anything for money. I was scared and insecure, and my search for decent and steady employment proved extremely difficult to secure. Not only did I not have the required "New York" work experience, I also hadn't acquired any skills beyond the basic knowledge of using a typewriter, a cash register, and answering a telephone. It was as if the doors to opportunity were shut and sealed tight, and I was barred and excluded from entering in.

As I look back on it, I don't blame them for not hiring me. This city offers plenty of job opportunities, yet those opportunities are also highly competitive. There was nothing to distinguish me from anybody else, or set me apart from any other applicant who was seeking that same position. If anything, they had more going for them, by having a college education and the skills of working in an urban environment such as this. At that point, I had acquired an Associate's Degree but hadn't yet earned the full four-year undergraduate degree, and the completion of a Bachelor's Degree was to make a significant difference.

Furthermore, I had very little knowledge of computers at that time, and without that, jobs are nil and next to nothing. I was just a stray who had haphazardly blown into the city. Perhaps I should have blown right back out, but I was also stubborn and determined, and I was never one to give up quickly. I'm the type who will fight it out until the tenth round; and only then, after a realistic analysis of the situation, will I let go. Let's face it: some things are just not meant to be.

At this time in my life, I didn't have much under my belt to make a name for myself without relying on the kindness of strangers. My path was not flat and straight; but rather, it seemed to veer off in countless and pointless directions, with side roads that led to dead ends. My road was not straight and narrow, and I did not experience ease of passage. It seemed I had an upward climb with a very heavy load on my back. Am I ever going to reach the top? It was like trying to scale a skyscraper, and there are lots of those in N.Y.C.

This is a view from the viewing platform of the Empire State Building in March of 1995; you can see the Twin Towers when they were standing (ORIGINAL IMAGE).

The Hard Knocks of the City

"Wigstock" July 1995 (New York). Even his poodle's fur was dyed blue!

My experience trying to establish myself in New York City was a most difficult undertaking indeed. The road was surely a bumpy one, with large rocks (like huge boulders) more often than not blocking my way. I tried everything that I could think of, but nothing seemed to work out. Every door I knocked on remained locked and sealed tight: Everything I touched turned to dust, and every road I went down led me to a dead end.

MY ARRIVAL TO NEW YORK CITY

That's when I thought I had no other option but to start stripping for a living. I would walk around Times Square (the way it was at that time) and pass by all the strip joints, nude bars, and adult movie houses. I went into a few, had on-the-spot interviews, and landed a job immediately every time. They didn't need computer knowledge, a college degree, or coin that "New York" work experience. All I needed was my body to do a strip tease or lap dance for lewd and bawdy men. But when they would say I could start that night, I would come as close as the front door, but then walk right on by.

I forgot the name of the last strip joint that hired me. I only recall talking to a man who merely took down my name and number and asked about my availability. He then gave me a see-through lacy thing to put on and said I would have to buy the shoes myself which had to be black and high heels. From there, I was pointed to a dimly-lit corner room where I was expected to put the thing on. There was absolutely nothing to it. A woman might as well walk around naked. I could crumple it up into a tiny ball with my fist, and I have small hands. I put the thing on and looked at myself in the mirror. It looked to me like I was completely nude except for a slight silky layer, like a milky film (more like a haze) that barely covered my bare skin, and attempted to obscure my body from the male gaze, while at the same time, an offer to tease. It appeared to bring my features out, making my breasts look big and busty, even voluptuous; which was a curious twist, because in reality, they are simply sufficient in size.

I remember not knowing what to do once I had put the thing on, so I just stood there waiting. There were a few young ladies near me who were also dressing for the evening. They looked just as naked as me. I noticed their shiny black high heels. I also noticed they were wearing black fishnet stockings whereas my legs were left bare. I assumed from this that it was also up to me to purchase the mesh nylons and panty hoses as well. I asked as to what we were supposed to do and was told that it was our job to serve drinks and "entertain" the men. I could stand on the raised platform and dance if I wanted to. The opportunity to do so would be most welcomed. At this point, I was given a little advice as to serving the men their drinks: If a man wanted to touch me, he was allowed to. It was my job to serve him his vodka, tequila, whiskey, brandy, or beer, and be there to please him. I must be a pleasure to see, to feel, and also to touch, if it is so desired. After all, the man is paying to be pleased.

I was having difficulty with the entire set-up of this situation. It reminded me of my time in Atlanta, serving drinks one night as a so-called cocktail waitress while wearing thin threads of silk and little pieces of lace. I would set their drinks down before them and notice their eyes go directly, immediately, to my butt and my breasts. I remember the requests to touch, the hands on my butt, and I especially recall how one man asked me to bend down close so that he could see my bare breasts underneath the silky covering. Most men, however, would just grab me in the ass without asking.

So, as I was about to walk out of the changing room dressed in see-through and hair-thin threads, I stood and thought for a long moment. I had vowed to myself to never again prance around in front of men with nothing but a piece of lace to cover my body. I had sworn that I would never allow myself to be so debased and demeaned ever again and I vowed to keep my promise. So I changed back into my street clothes and walked out.

VIEWING PLATFORM OF the Empire State Building (March 1995) "Burlesque" Filter.

Between a Rock and a Hard Place

This was "Wigstock" in New York back in July of 1995.

It was tough getting life started in New York City. Frank Sinatra was right when he sang in his song *"New York, New York"* that if you can make it here, then you can make it anywhere. Seriously, he wasn't kidding! And to think that I always thought that those were simply lyrics to an old song. Little did I know that one day I would live that same song in my own life!

I was able to land a few odd jobs like house cleaning or dog walking; and later, a few temporary office positions, but I made very little money. I taught myself to use a computer and learned Microsoft Word at my receptionist job in an attempt to combat boredom. I typed my thoughts and played with fonts to keep myself awake. I was still desperate for housing and in between roommates, I stayed with either John or Ray. I met guys at bars or clubs, or through ads in the Village Voice of an all-male band looking for a female lead singer. I can't explain why I wanted so much to be a singer/songwriter, except to say that it attracts much of our culture's youth. Many young people come from all over to New York City to be in the spotlight and to have their chance to shine. My eyes dazzled at the prospect of having a life of fame and fortune, and being loved and admired. And New York is the perfect place for such magic can happen.

Yet that magic wasn't happening as quickly as I wanted it to, or were things turning out the way I had expected them to. I didn't find that perfect band to perform with or land that record deal that I just assumed was due me. The truth is, I was stage-shy: I had no musical talent whatsoever, and I couldn't even sing in the first place. The men I stayed with along the way of my trying to become some "Superstar Rockstar" were mostly taking me in for reasons of their own. Not all of them made these intentions known, and not every one of them just wanted to bed me. Some actually wanted to be my boyfriend. A few just wanted to be friends. I don't remember most of them and perhaps that's for the best. I don't think I would want to recall all those faces. I can still see fuzzy pictures of faces from a vague point in the past but with no names. I also have similarly obscure pictures of places where I had once stayed but with no faces.

Meeting these men and crashing on their couch was my way of survival for the first year. For two years after that, my living arrangements were a wee bit more stable. I mostly stayed with two of the men I met, each for an extended period of time. One was Ray, the other John, who I met in Central Park one hot day in July. He worked in the film industry and was setting up lights for a shoot to a movie scene as I sat resting after having walked blocks to get a job. Ray was to become one of my best friends, while John was a friend only for that time.

I lived in each of the 5 boroughs - Manhattan, Brooklyn, Queens - (I live in The Bronx) and stayed awhile on Staten Island. I had many roommate situations: mostly with men, sometimes with women; most times with other singles, but a couple times with a married couple. I rented the spare room of a loft from two guys who were gay and shared an apartment above a kitchen cabinet store with a woman who was a lesbian. It seemed I was either working at low-paying odd jobs while trying to get permanent employment, or I was seeking yet another place to live. Those three years proved themselves to be most difficult indeed. I was not at all prepared for the rejection from jobs that I received. I also was not prepared for the constant onslaught of cat-calls and crude comments that I got from men on the street. The hard knocks of the city caused damage to the confidence I once had, to the positive attitude and attributes that I had claimed for myself, and they practically destroyed my self-esteem.

During these times, I felt I was between a rock and a hard place. My attempts to get out of these situations often turned into desperation, and I started to seriously doubt my purpose in life and question the very reason for my existence. I began to believe that I was a nobody who deserved no goodness to come to me and even doubted I had a soul. I was lost, fearful, frustrated, and confused. At one point, I thought to jump off a seventh-floor fire escape, because I was so overwhelmed and broken-hearted over a boy. But I figured it significantly worse if I survived and ended up paralyzed, so I held back and refrained. Instead, I leaned back against the stiff brick of the building and thought for a long moment. I looked up at the darkness and blackness of the summer night sky. I stared straight at the white moon until I got too tired to think and just wanted to sleep. I climbed through the window and went back inside.

**Viewing platform of the Empire State Building (March 1995)
"Sunscreen" Filter.**

BLANK PAGE

Chapter 05: My Adjustment to Life in New York

[This describes my experience of transitioning and acclimating to the Big Apple that is New York. It takes a lot to adjust to a big city when you come from a small Midwestern town. The process can be a sluggish one, despite the fact that you launch at full speed and hit the ground running. With challenges to face and obstacles to overcome, my adjustment was definitely not easy for me.]

I'm dark in this picture, but I like the big city scene behind me.

Blood and Bone versus Concrete and Steel

He was very handsome in person: This picture did him no justice! This photo is from July 1995. I am 22 years old, a month shy of 23.

I WAS IN A FIERCE GAME of tug-of-war with New York City. That is really the best way that I can describe it. The city did not exactly open its arms warmly and wide to welcome and receive me, or roll out the red carpet and serve the wine. Most people softly knock and doors open for them; I have to loudly pound and even kick the doors down. The city could be cold and cruel indeed, but I must admit: It has the most spectacular skyline at night!

In time, I got myself more together, though there were still plenty of things to contend with. After months of searching, I got a job working in a group home on West 14th Street in Manhattan for mentally-challenged and developmentally-disabled adults, which didn't require prior New York work experience or even a college degree for that matter. The pay was very low and the hours were long, but it was full-time and steady, and I couldn't complain.

I worked with six other young women who were all in college and worked part-time, and it was our job to counsel the six developmentally-disabled ladies who lived on site at the residence. We were to teach them independent living skills and to assist them with integrating into the community. It sounds more than what it was. What it boiled down to was making sure that they arrived safely to their appointments and destinations, and getting dinner ready every evening. Most importantly, we had to make sure that everybody got along. That was of paramount importance. It was more like babysitting and childminding than actual counseling. But it was full-time and steady, and still I could not complain.

My co-workers all went to Hunter College. I thought about going back to get my Bachelor's degree, but I didn't know where to go or what to go for. I heard that the C.U.N.Y. (City University of New York) educational system was affordable and respectable (it's got about 25 colleges located throughout the city's five boroughs), and Hunter College was considered to be one of the best. I wasn't ready to return to school right then, but I knew I had to go back eventually in order to be marketable and to make more money.

I didn't go back to school right then. Instead, after leaving the job at the group home for a receptionist position, I did temp work and also had more temporary living arrangements. For example, I had a small room for rent in the basement of a house in Brooklyn. Ray called me "Mole Woman." John called it the "Welfare Hotel." There was the family pitbull that kept its face in my small square window; a bathroom so small it seemed more like an outhouse, and the steam pipe that was on the verge of bursting just above my bed.

I finally managed to land my own apartment in Queens, which was when I left the permanent position with the low hourly wage at the group home for the temporary one that paid more. I'm not sure if the financial trade-off outweighed the benefit of permanent employment, but I thought it a smart move at the time. But after my roommate left me with a big mess and stiffed me with a phone bill (almost $350 dollars!) I stayed with Ray, and later, John once again.

At the time, I changed the color of my hair to jet black. I thought having dark black hair that contrasted against my pale white skin would make me strikingly beautiful! In reality, it only made me look sick and washed out. I guess the "gothic babe" look just wasn't for me. I don't know why I wanted black hair, but now looking back on it, I was going through a lot of hardship and pain. In a way, the black in my hair represented the black in my heart: It was the darkness I felt inside my soul. I also dressed in black and blue – entirely unconsciously, yet now that I look back on it: It was almost as if to resemble a walking bruise. In many ways, it seemed to divulge and disclose my overall sadness and distress.

Life in New York City was proving to be very hard. I thought I was going to take the city by storm, but as time went on and days turned into years, it appeared to me that the city was hell-bent on beating me up and taking me by storm instead. The theme from "New York, New York" would play in my head. *"If I can make it here, I'll make it anywhere"* Frank Sinatra sings. Perhaps he knew how hard it was too! But I didn't want to just subsist and survive: I wanted to flourish pond even thrive! Hard work was not even half of it: It takes a lot of green Irish luck – and a whole lot more green money! It was a battle between flesh and blood versus concrete and steel. If this was a tug-of-war being waged between the two of us, at this point, N.Y.C. was definitely winning!

This is a view from the viewing platform of the Empire State Building in March of 1995: You can see Central Park in the background (this is the ORIGINAL IMAGE).

From Roommates to Dorm Rooms

This was "Wigstock" back in July of 1995, New York City.

Finding affordable housing was a never-ending contest and challenge for me in New York City. In fact, it turned out to be a thorn in my side and the bane of my existence. I struggled with housing issues practically the entire time I lived in N.Y.C. During this early period, I had many roommates, of which two stand out in particular: Josh and Scott. Both were very difficult to live with, but each for a different reason.

My roommate, Josh, had an apartment in Washington Heights along the upper west side of Manhattan. It was his apartment, and he ran it like a tight ship. He was so uptight that he wanted me to clean the toaster after every use! After each slice of bread that I toasted, the toaster had to be wiped clean. He had a cat that would puke all the time, and he was adamant about not leaving cat puke on the carpet. He would say that whoever was around when the cat got sick or threw up a hairball, then that person needed to clean it off the carpet before it settled in and made a stain. I swear it only puked when I was home. It really irritated me to be continually cleaning up after his cat.

He had a thing too with the dishes. He'd make a big mess in the kitchen, but if I so much as left just three dishes in the sink, he would throw a temper. He would gather them up and put them out onto the fire escape. Then, after he was done with his own sloppy mess, he would put them back in the sink, so that I'd have to clean my cup, bowl, and spoon myself. He also was obsessive and compulsive about creating lists of who buys what and when, and for how much. For example: If he bought toilet paper, he would write his initials and the price (down to the cent) on a notepad and stick it to the refrigerator in order to keep us reminded as to who was buying what. He asked me to do the same, but I never would. But then, when I would buy things and not list them, he would list them for me, putting my initials and the price of the paper towels I bought on a yellow sticky note next to his.

He could be so cocky and rude. The only time I had a change of mind was one summer night in the wee hours of the morning, when some guy just kept setting somebody's car alarm off on the street. It must have been around 3 A.M., and the guy just kept kicking this person's car, and the alarm would sound loud enough for the entire street block to hear. Josh got so angry that he ran to the refrigerator, grabbed a carton of eggs, and quickly went back to his bedroom. He opened the window all the way to the top and started to pellet the man with the eggs. I stood at his bedroom door and watched him whip one after another by taking good aim first, and then throwing it with all his might.

"I almost got him!" he shouted to me with a smile stretched wide across his face, and for a moment, I thought he was cool. But for the most part, he was pretty moody. Walking on his eggshells made me nervous, so within just a few short months, I moved out.

I moved in with Scott so that I could move out from Josh. Scott lived along Kings Highway in Brooklyn. We discussed his room for rent over a glass of water with classical music playing quietly in the background. He seemed laid-back and easy-going, and I thought he would make a good roommate to live with... then I moved in. I should have expected the change. He didn't drink cups of water but rather seemed to turn into an alcoholic overnight. He liked his vodka every evening straight out of the bottle. He used to come home stumbling drunk. It got to be uncomfortable for me and I wanted to have a lock put on my bedroom door. But it wasn't just that, although that would have been plenty reason to leave. He also played his music really loud. I'd be in my room, the door shut, the window open and my music on, and still hear every beat and sound of his. He blasted heavy-metal death-jam as loud as it could go, and it just got to be too much for me. I may crave the crazy busy of these city streets, but I still need a quiet place to rest and to call my home.

In my eagerness to move out, I stayed with some women I met at a church I had just started attending. It was the summer I was definite about returning to school. I had been in New York for almost three years at this point. I stayed with Michelle and her two roommates in a tiny apartment in Manhattan, and also with her friend, Vicky, and her two roommates as well. I really liked living in Manhattan, because it felt like I was in the very epicenter of everything! The experience of it was very inspiring and exciting! But I didn't like the costly, cramped, crowded, and closed-in space of their apartment, and I especially didn't like all the cockroaches that came out at night.

MY ARRIVAL TO NEW YORK CITY

I clearly remember when I turned on the light late one night to get a quick drink of water, and cockroaches scattered everywhere. I was so scared that I stood there for a second frozen still until running out of the room. Once I was taking a shower, and when I opened my eyes after I rinsed my hair, I saw a few on the shower curtain, and one climbing down the spout just above my head. It felt like I lived in a roach motel. Within a few months, I got accepted into the Hunter dormitory and I was very happy to be out of that place.

Starting college again for the second time was a whole new beginning for me. I already had earned my Associate's degree back in Michigan, and I now was determined to earn my Bachelor's. It gave me a goal to focus on, and I set my sights on the degree that in three years I would achieve. I no longer needed to work at odd jobs and sleep on couches or in make-shift bedrooms with just a curtain for a door. Life did not turn suddenly rosy – believe me! – but returning to college and living in a dormitory did succeed in planting and grounding me when I needed it most. It steadied and stabilized me at a time when I was really floundering to find my footing, and that was exactly what I needed.

It was now August of 1996, and I felt both excitement and trepidation about returning to college. My excitement was due to the change in my life that was about to occur, which was a change I was eager for and that needed to take place, yet my fear was just as strong. Because in order for me to return to college, I needed the money to go; and to get it, I had to take out a student loan which scared me very much. I didn't want to owe anybody, and I didn't want to have to pay back a large sum of money with interest either.

Yet my life had to change. Every road I traveled down brought me to a dead end. It felt I had no other choice. I wished to be free from the hardship and difficulty that continued to bombard and beset me. I needed a life that offered plenty of opportunity; one that would allow me to open doors and step through and see the possibilities that existed just beyond the other side, but that were currently closed to me and completely out of my reach. I wanted to compete in the job market; and for that, you really need a college degree. A high school diploma alone typically is not enough to provide that competitive edge. It's a combination of work experience and higher education that opens doors to future (and better) offers of employment. I wanted a fresh start and a new beginning: a chance to put the hardships of my past away and to begin again. I wanted to be happy – yes, triumphant! – and I yearned to find me.

Viewing platform of the Empire State Building (March 1995) "Sahara" Filter.

The Empire State Building has 103 floors. Its construction was commenced in 1930 – and it was completed in just one year!

This is a view from the viewing platform of the Empire State Building
on March of 1995. The tower lights up in different colors according to
the holiday, season or occasion, and the lights always go off at 2 a.m.

Empire State Building, March 1995. You can see Central Park behind me.

I was with my friend Ray. He was the one taking the pictures.
Viewing platform of the Empire State Building (March of 1995).
He was using my old 35 mm camera with actual roles of film.

Ray took this picture of me (Empire State Building) March 1995.
You can see both the Hudson River and New Jersey behind me.

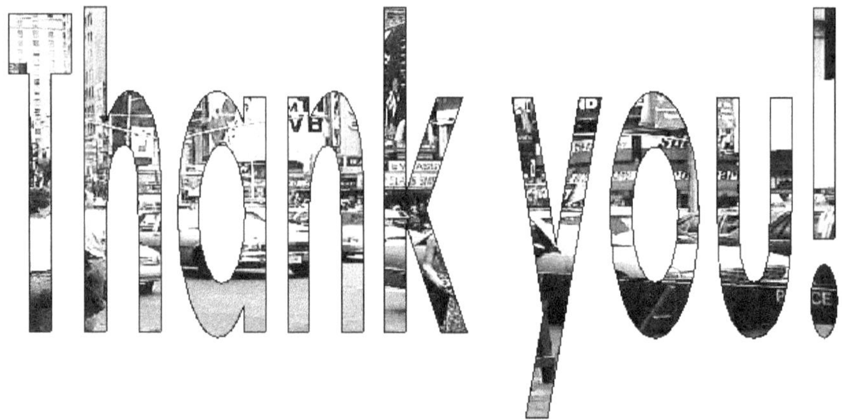
Thank you!

for reading my book.

I really appreciate it!

DELYNN NICOLE POMA

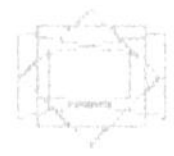

54

Don't miss out!

Visit the website below and you can sign up to receive emails whenever DeLynn Nicole Poma publishes a new book. There's no charge and no obligation.

https://books2read.com/r/B-A-NBRX-HZSNC

BOOKS 2 READ

Connecting independent readers to independent writers.

Did you love *My Arrival to (and Early Life in) New York City*? Then you should read *My First Night in New York City*[1] by DeLynn Nicole Poma!

This is the story of how I arrived to New York City. This is the beginning in documenting and describing my experience in starting a new life inside the mega-metropolis that is New York. This piece is super short and includes a few images as well. It is not meant to provide an in-depth retelling or account about my time inside the Big Apple; but rather, it is intended to serve as a short recap of that first night. The real story is told through the letters and journals I wrote at that time. For now, this is simply a snapshot description about my impetuous, impulsive, and impromptu arrival to N.Y.C.

---

1. https://books2read.com/u/m2qDpj

2. https://books2read.com/u/m2qDpj

Also by DeLynn Nicole Poma

New York City
My First Night in New York City
My Early Days in New York City
My Early Years in New York City
My Early Days and Years in New York City
My Adjustment to Life in New York City
My Arrival to (and Early Life in) New York City

Standalone
My Youthful Atlanta Days

About the Author

HELLO!! My name is Lynn and I have been writing privately for many years. Recently, I've been asking myself: "What's the point of all that writing if it stays hidden on my computer and no one ever reads it?" Therefore, I have decided to make my writing public and self-publish it. Admittedly, organizing what has become a mountain of writing is a daunting task indeed, but one I am committed to investing time in.

Honestly, my goal was never to be a writer. It's not so much that I like to write as it is my need to get thought out of my head (it helps me to think more clearly). I spend/waste no time on drafts, and what comes out stays on the page with little or no editing. I wish I could have been a pianist or painter (even a dancer!), something that is musical or visual. Alas, writing chose me; and so, I'm collecting pieces I have written over the years and putting them into e-book/print form.

THANK YOU!! for purchasing/downloading and reading my title! I hope you enjoyed it. I truly do appreciate it. 😊 😊 😊